C000225136

SPRINGS OF HAPPINESS

Bacon
Bulwer
Franklin
Grenfell
Thoreau
Yeats

NO PLEASURE
IS COMPARABLE
TO THE
STANDING UPON
THE
VANTAGE-GROUND
OF TRUTH·

FRANCIS BACON

In spite of all
our wanderings
HAPPINESS
is always found within
a narrow
compass
and among objects
which lie within
our immediate reach.

BULWER

The fate of man prepares happy moments, not happy times.

NIETZSCHE

Happiness begins for us
when we have put an end
to our pretensions-
for they bring us, after all,
nothing but
pain and discomfort.

CHAMFORT

If man succeeds
in removing suffering
with pills and drops,
then he will
completely ignore
religion and philosophy,
in which he has
so far found not only
help
against all affliction
but even happiness.

A. CHEKHOV

HAPPINESS IS LIKE
A SUNBEAM,
WHICH THE LEAST
SHADOW
INTERCEPTS.

CHINESE PROVERB

No-one can forge a life-time
of happiness, only ever
the happiness of the moment.

WAGGERL

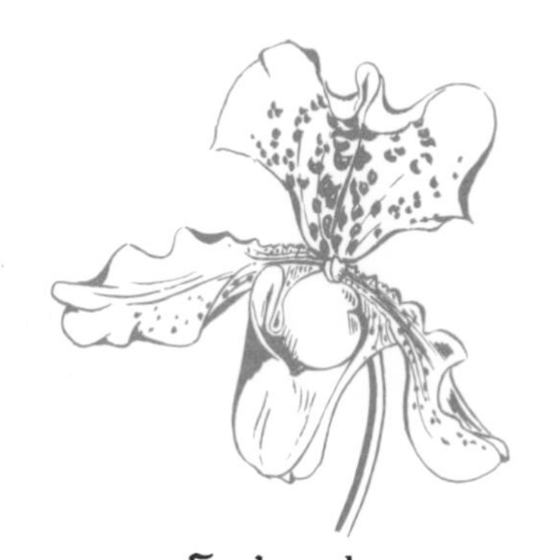

Seek not
to have that everything
should happen as you wish,
but wish for everything
to happen
as it actually does happen,
and you will be serene.

EPICTETUS

An hour of
concentrated work
does more to kindle joy,
to overcome sadness
and to set
your ship afloat again,
than a month
of
gloomy brooding.

BENJAMIN FRANKLIN

Your joy is
your sorrow unmasked.
And the selfsame
well from which your
laughter rises
was oftentimes filled
with your tears.

KAHLIL GIBRAN

The supreme happiness of life
is the conviction that we are loved.
VICTOR HUGO

TO CONQUER A JOY IS MORE VALUABLE THAN GIVING ONESELF UP TO A SORROW.

ANDRÉ GIDE

WHAT IS THE USE
OF LOVE,
GOOD FORTUNE,
KNOWLEDGE AND RICHES,
IF YOU DO NOT GIVE
YOURSELF TIME
TO ENJOY THEM
IN LEISURE.

GLEICHEN-RUSSWURM

GENUINE JOY GROWS
NOT
FROM CONTEMPLATION,
NOT FROM RICHES
AND NOT FROM FAME,

BUT FROM WORK
THAT HAS ITS OWN
INNER VALUE.

WILFRED GRENFELL

God has more love and mercy
than a man can ever sin against.

N. LENAU

Serenity is neither frivolity,
nor complacency,
it is the highest knowledge
and love,
it is the affirmation of all reality
being awake at the edge
of all deeps and abysses.
Serenity is the secret of beauty
and the real substance
of all art.

HERMANN HESSE

What a man is to himself,
what accompanies him into
solitude,
and what no-one can give him
or take away from him,
this is evidently
more important to him than
everything he may possess
or
what he is in the eyes of others.

SCHOPENHAUER

Those undeserved
joys which come
uncalled and make
us more pleased
than grateful
are they that sing.

HENRY DAVID THOREAU

That is the mystery of grace:
it never comes too late.
FRANÇOIS MAURIAC

We shall never plumb
the depths and
the ultimate mysteries
of life.
The only thing
that really matters
is what we make
of our lives.

THORNTON WILDER

In wise love
each divines the high secret
self of the other,
and, refusing to believe
in the mere daily self,
creates a mirror
where the lover
or the beloved
sees an image to copy
in daily life.

W. B. YEATS

Precious little gifts of lasting value

In the same series:
SPRINGS OF COMFORT
SPRINGS OF LOVE
SPRINGS OF FRIENDSHIP
SPRINGS OF HOPE
SPRINGS OF INDIAN WISDOM
SPRINGS OF JAPANESE WISDOM
SPRINGS OF MUSIC
SPRINGS OF ORIENTAL WISDOM
SPRINGS OF PERSIAN WISDOM
SPRINGS OF JOY
SPRINGS OF JEWISH WISDOM
AFFECTION, FRIENDSHIP AND LOVE
IN PRAISE OF BEAUTY
SPRINGS OF CHINESE WISDOM
SPRINGS OF ROMAN WISDOM
SPRINGS OF ANIMAL WISDOM
SPRINGS OF STILLNESS AND SOLITUDE

Acknowledgements: Illustations: flowers
by Klaus Meyer-Gasters / Weisbecker-Verlag, Frankfurt

Text chosen by E. Hettinger
Translated by Dr. Peter M. Daly

Distribution:
UK: Search Press Ltd. England
USA: National Book Network Inc. Lanham/Maryland

Printed in Switzerland